Witness

poems (Hollywood 7/06)

For Jodi & Andy — With love! Lorraine

Lorraine Stanchich

Epic
Press

Belleville, Ontario, Canada

Witness

Copyright © 2003, Lorraine Stanchich

Cover art and illustrations by Michael Grosso

"When You Love a Mafia Soldier" appeared in *The Journal of New Jersey Poets*, Autumn 1999.

Thanks to Robert Carnevale for his encouragement and very generous support of this work.

National Library of Canada Cataloguing in Publication

Stanchich, Lorraine, 1968-

      Witness : poems / Lorraine Stanchich.

ISBN 1-55306-568-9

      I. Title.

PS3619.T354W58 2003   811'.6   C2003-900262-4

**For more information or
to order additional copies, please contact:**
Lorraine Stanchich
P.O. Box 254
Vernon, NJ 07462 USA
landoflorraine.com

Epic Press is an imprint of *Essence Publishing*. For more information, contact:
44 Moira Street West, Belleville, Ontario, Canada K8P 1S3
Phone: 1-800-238-6376 • Fax: (613) 962-3055
E-mail: info@essencegroup.com • Internet: www.essencegroup.com

For Jack

Testis unus testis nullus

One witness is no witness

—anon

Contents

Giovanna 9

His Nakedness 14

Di. 15

Oscars. 18

Absentia 20

One Jesus 22

Wedding Day 26

The Boy who Survived Hitler. 28

Gravity 32

Vietnam. 33

Dizzy's Last Gig 34

Gringa in Her Own Home 36

When You Love a Mafia Soldier 39

Fall on the Lake. 41

The Fact 43

First Husband 45

Sisters 47

Procedure 50

Patterns 52

Kuwait 54

Where Are You Headed? 57

Postcard 62

Peruvian-Yugoslavian-Italian-American 64

Corporate Epiphany #365 67

Crossing Over Loss 69

Go 72

Lakeside, Month Eight 74

Spring Lake 76

About the Author 78

About the Artist 79

Giovanna

On a Yugoslavian farm,
she was born at dawn.
The oxen puffed and steamed nearby.
Crying, she stretched into the straw.
She was fifth
behind four brothers.

At nine,
she asked them
how babies were born.
They laughed roughly
as they slaughtered the dinner hens
and milked the cow.

At nineteen,
as she served breakfast,

Mussolini paraded by
and the boys ran in the road
to see who could touch
his passing car.

At twenty-nine,
she bailed hay,
milked the cow, and plowed the land
by hand, wondering when the Italian Navy
would allow her husband a leave.
She wondered and cried as she knelt
in the dirt.

At thirty-nine,
she was torn from his shirt
as stoic soldiers in green suits
took the men to labor camps.
She carried grain
fifty miles
to feed her sons.

One morning, while eating shoe leather
in broth,
she turned forty-nine,
and the bombs exploded around her

like broken hearts.
When her boys weren't witnessing
executions behind thin shrubbery,
she read to them.

II.

In a misty port,
she arrived at dawn.
Crying, she undertook America.
In an Italian deli in West New York,
she was five thousand miles
behind her brothers.
At fifty-nine, she asked God,
"How come?"
She laughed roughly as she
swatted the mice out of her
crammed pantry
and sent her grandchildren
to overstock it more.

At sixty-nine,
as she served breakfast,
her faithful transistor radio buzzed
Carter's pleas about the gas
while the boys ran in the street

among parked cars.
One morning,
while eating anisette toast with
black coffee,
she turned seventy-nine,
and when her sons
weren't hiding from their torments,
they read to her.

III.

At eighty-nine,
she lay dying in a New Jersey hospital.
I arrived at dawn.
Crying, she stretched her arm towards mine.
She said, on a Yugoslavian farm,
she was fifth
behind four brothers—
names and faces she no longer knew.
She asked me
how babies were born.
I looked at her,
drew in a defiant breath,
and laughed roughly
to make her feel at home.

His Nakedness

There was something so indelibly real—
His nakedness was speaking to me
this morning. As he rose, I didn't steal
a look at his penis—it just suddenly
showed itself, and glowed in the misty dawn light
like a baby awakening. I stared,
unobsessed, as if looking from a height
I knew I couldn't reach—something we shared
yet so totally his. Not a word was spoken,
while my untamed locks sprawled on a white sheet,
tangled in my arms, with his smell—my brief token
of many dawns like this: body complete
with the luxuriance of a sated tryst.
Then he went to dress; my eyes closed to resist.

Di

She died at the worst time:
at the height of love, beauty,
celebrity. Wearing fur
to funerals while despairing
with musicians, making
childbirth chic—I always
wanted to live like this. She
got that stroke of odd luck,
making history for marrying
a royal asshole—getting
a personal astrologer and
beautician for her trouble.
There were days she looked so sad—
Yet so demure—in a pretty pink suit
and matching pillbox hat,
you could only love her
stylish sulking all the more.

During my divorce, I wanted
to die—didn't stand a chance
of being glamorous about it.
There was no staff to say,
"You go girl," or to adorn
my aching anima with the right
cream taffeta gown, no
matching shoes for the heavy-footed
underdog I was that year.

So when she went, all my hopes
for losing gracefully
went too, and I swear
I almost bought a ticket
to Britain just so I could
add a bouquet of red roses
to the piles mounting
at her mansion, just to get
closer to the country her corpse
was in—if someone from TV
got me on camera, crying
while placing my flowers down,
Di would have been
a plausible part of me—

and maybe I wouldn't have to die
knowing that misfortune
is, in fact, unfashionable.

Oscars

As I approach the tank
to change their water,
the Tiger Oscars dash to the glass,
in search of food.
Fighting each other to the hood,
they stir orange and brown debris.
As my well-meaning arm
enters their world, all at once
they turn betrayed: listless,
common, pale, dismayed. They drop
from top to bottom in disgust,
loathing, losing their swank. This
transformation is inert—
They are in prison, and as my hand
dislodges the rotten gunk and waste,
they back up against the glass, inept;
no longer cocky, but beat. No longer

in their own universe, but in mine.
Their philosophic stares hurry my act;
their languid, incarcerated glares
make me rush to restore
uprooted plants and stones; to lessen
their mistrust and return their home—
Prove to them I love them,
that these scars are all for their welfare.
But each time, they fall and pale
and never learn again;
as if each week when I clean their reef
I'm removing their names.

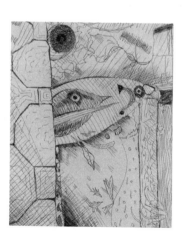

Absentia

Everything about my father has to do with his surviving the war:
The pine table in our dining room reminds him of the farmhouse
Where they fled, the meals they ate there as sparse as the furnishings.

Every occasion is an occasion to remember, all in tragic pleasantry—
The hills in Warwick remind him of the Slavic hills the Germans
Advanced down, at, and into his home, his grandparents' homes,
His uncles' homes, his cousins' rooms, the pictures on the walls.

Every moment—sharing an apple, reminds him of the apples
He didn't have, or the apple he got, when he tended the sheep and
An uncle remembered a birthday, bestowing the shiny yellow fruit
Like a prize trophy gotten in exchange for blood.

Every baby born in my family is the child he could never afford
To be, we could never be, the children he saw dying in the streets,
Hiding in the brush, crying hoarse through gunfire.

Every phone call is a strain to make him think I understand, to
Love him through my American Absentia—to say it's okay
You aren't with me, you never were, even when you tried.

Every day I love him more, I lose him more, our worlds
Parting like pared fruit, falling into different hands.
Every second of my life, I long for him in a way he should know well.
He is a man of history, who remembers.

One Jesus

Before September 11th,
a mother only had
one Jesus in her heart: He
who blessed her with a son—
not the one who could
allow one sunny morning
to be the backdrop for the end
of her child's life.

She couldn't help herself—
her disbelieving cries, her
failed attempts to avoid looking
at Jesus differently.
she remembered the One
who looked in on her
when she bode her time

between an ideal
and an unborn child,

when all she could do
was thank Him. Look
at my baby's fingers, his
pursed lips, cellophane eyelids,
fingers gripping a trembling
hand, his pure breath.

The wonder never waned.
Those fragile fingers
turned to strong hands; little legs
to a soccer player's strong legacy.
Her greatest joy was his
kindness. So it made no sense,
it couldn't be that Jesus
she thought she knew, when

this investment banker
turned to ash in an instant
at the hands of someone
a world away.
That one Jesus

was only there for the birth,
she bitterly mourned. Jesus
would have honored those years,
the wiped tears and the skinned
knees and all the diapers and
lost sleep and lessons taught and

lessons learned. That first step,
that first school day, that
first girl who chased him
into the woods for a kiss. No—
that one Jesus wasn't there
for this. A wrinkled, graying,
ragged mother hated this

Jesus who she couldn't
understand, who stole her
son who had become such
a good man. She hated
the very idea of her beloved
son sacrificed in the
Third World War: she

thought hard at Jesus:

the one she exalted

as her beautiful boy lay in her

unsteady arms 31 years ago,

and the one from September 11th,

who laid her son down

in unsteady buildings.

Wedding Day

We were leaning
side by side in the mirror,
when my hands were trembling too much.
You put down your red lipstick
and abandoned yourself to the task
of holding my chin with authority,
and applying my makeup—
sweeping just the right browns
across my flitting lids, putting powder
all over the lines. Then you blew
twice in my face, sized me up
with blue, determined eyes,
and started my mascara. You smeared
the lip gloss on. You brushed sparkle powder
across my breasts. You dried
the tears before they fell. You said
relax, it's going to be okay,

but how would you know?
I always dragged you off the avenue,
nights when your knees buckled
under your drunk weight,
your platinum blond hair hung
over your face like a wet mop.
You'd fight me under street lamps
saying let me go, this guy's okay.
All those countless moments
I chose you first, when you never
chose yourself.
Finally it came that I hit you,
and you couldn't move your neck
for a week. You blamed me
for your pains, and all I could do
was wish we were back to
my wedding day, you squeezing
my hand while I whispered my vows.

The Boy who Survived Hitler

Croatia, 1944

Dread occurred like an impulsive current as he played on the porch of his grandfather's farmhouse. As if awakened from a dream, he looked up and squinted through the sun at the green mountains above the townlet. The hills were moving: up and over and down the peaks and valleys of his youth came the soldiers. They swarmed toward him, little boy, wide-eyed, mussed hair, barefoot in the dust.

"Wasser! Wasser!" They demanded, and since from his grandparents the boy knew some German, he ran inside to fetch their water. The look on his face as he swung into the kitchen was all his grandmother needed to see. Her hands gripped a vase and trembled as she filled it with water.

The soldiers drank in gulps as the water ran down their necks, the froth from their mouths bubbling over the rims of the cups. Their large guns clinked against their belts as the water darkened their uniforms to an even deeper green. The boy waited, blinking, while the swarms moved into the village, burning houses and hanging the neighbors. Uncle Pepito, who only moments before had been pulling weeds in front of his house, swayed from the large oak tree in his yard as if from heaven—puppeted by a yellow rope around his neck, face still in the conundrum of how to kill the weeds below him.

Larger, fair-skinned boys were automatically taken from their homes and put into the Army. Any sick or crippled were shot immediately. There was no time to think. The boy's cousin, who was visiting from next door, had a permanent limp from playing with a grenade when he was three. Now four, and fearing the soldiers, he stumbled silently into the folds of his grandmother's skirt as the soldiers stormed into the house.

The little cousin clung to his grandmother's leg under the dark gray cloth, thinking of it as a theater curtain.
She reacted suddenly and briskly, serving the soldiers

fresh borscht and cheese; she moved efficiently through her kitchen as if serving just another meal; she waited on them as she spoke German as hospitably and as stealthily as if it were her native tongue.

Sweat formed in patches on her large, white thighs, then dripped as she worked: salty rivulets streamed from her waist—small deadly cascades challenging the little cousin's grip. He regrouped, digging his nails into her with all his strength as she shuffled from stove to table with no misstep, her voice confident and cordial as she bent to lay bread on the table, her brother swaying outside her window.

The little cousin clutched hard in her dark folds during the soldiers' long reprieve. Her legs shaped his hands, the smell of her girdle snaps; her salty, wet legs, and the dense smell of her vagina were his life. There in her safety he heard the screaming surrounding the meal—men, women, babies, horses, rabbits, hogs. They all sounded the same.

Nothing would ever attract the senses again for the little cousin. He became a continual bystander to days like these, over and over until finally he merely existed as a witness, undone, unraveling into a certain bleary-eyed wisdom. He became a man who carried a looming omnipresence, bestowing tales of survival onto those he loved like terrible trophies.

Gravity

Every laugh remembers
the way you left my life,
reminds me of all you won't
experience with me: I think
of the person I wanted you to be.

I wish I could prevent
the ambush of my face, the smile
I can't erase, the ease.
I wish I could forget my love,
how much you mean to me.

Every laugh refutes
how we were welded
by this world, forsaken
for each other as the sky
endures the sea:

each one perceiving
the place where it should be.

Vietnam

The countryside
has lush green fields; we quest and comb
the countryside.
Inhabitants stand near their huts,
in every face, a native poem,
every life, a dark song. We roam
the countryside.

Dizzy's Last Gig

There's no way to know
when you're doing your last
gig. But I think Dizzy did.
Bobbling on thin legs,
his broad belly sucked in;
what came out through those
little lips ripped through the room—
puffy cheeks like cherry bombs blew
altitudes of love, searing and splendid.

With each whistle he looked wide-eyed,
straight at us, surprised and knowing.
Every blare was fanfare—the highest
place my heart could go.
Shrieks expanded into sighs:
his breath moved in rising swells, so
we couldn't speak. Some kids

said WOW and their parents
harshly rearranged them in their seats:
if you moved, you might miss
his horn—this thin, yellow piece
shoring up the enormity of Dizzy's world
with three buttons.

He burst an exalted bellow in the shiny,
gold hole, paused for a second and looked
sadly over our heads. Then he walked away.

Silence stood on the stage.
We went home, wiping
the sweat from our brows.

Gringa in Her Own Home

"Como te va?" Says her mother;
"Ok," She mutters,
half-knowing who she is today –
like one of those
fish in the pet shop, all pretty
in purple and red, ready to
take on the world, yet stuck
in a glass looking out, looking
for someone to let her swim
farther.

She is blonde, like her father,
with green eyes and light skin.
She shops with her abuelita in
West New York and is ignored
by the salesladies; they have
as much patience for Spanglish

as a suit to a beggar; they gab
ferociously forward, over the
counters and in between racks
relating to the latest gossip in
the telenovelas. Abuelita makes
a purchase for her nena because
no one will wait on her.

Back home in Northern New Jersey,
she volunteers at her church
distributing clothes to the Mexican
migrant workers, trying to speak
to them empathetically. Their
demeanor is restricted,
restrained. They don't
trust this Spanish either –
for reasons as different as
her parents – who came to America
only to find provinciality
more expansive and far-reaching
than their homelands, yet would
die before admitting it, even to
themselves.

"Por que no me contestas en Español?"

Her mother impatiently chides.

"No se, mom. I don't know."

When You Love a Mafia Soldier

Call a 12-hour drive
To a half-hour lunch
In a crowded, maximum-security
Prison cafeteria
Thanksgiving.
     Don't flinch at anything.
Say good-bye, I love you, and wait.
     Keep your money in the mattress
     Or out of state.
Get a gun when the money runs low.
     Yearn for everyone you know.
Sleep with the light on, keep windows locked.
(If it's summer, use a fan).
     Be the very doorjamb.
If your demands meet silence, thank God for the void.
     Keep many bank accounts
     Though you're unemployed.

Smile mutely at the neighbors from your
Suburban sprawl.
Field untimely, threatening telephone calls.
Shower with your eyes open—don't sing.
Keep them open—in a taxi, at the dentist,
At everything.
Choose sentimentality to override your hate.
When you are summoned at any time
Never—don't ever
Be late.

Fall on the Lake

An acorn falls from a tree and pops to the deck
among swirling winds and leaves
yellows and reds falling
and the acorn, helpless, nothing but a seed,
never growing, always knowing
all it won't be.

One by one
they hit the rocks by the water's edge,
chanceless in their round misery
inept as lost friends
creating ripples in blackness.
If you could hear one cry,

looking up at its tree
that's left its fruit to die
unborn, cover your ears!

The acorn dangles,

with no one to blame,

unable to brace itself for another day.

The Fact

Being Yugoslavian-American
is a game of reality juggling:
the trick is to be as American as possible—
be sure not to miss the season's
folk festivals, keep your child's
playdates, and look at minivan
catalogs for driving options. Succumbing

too far into other cultures can be risky:
Zoloft can be corrective for thinking
on the raped little girls in Bosnia
too often, and it couldn't hurt
to put a two-mile walk for
contaminated water out of your mind
when you turn on the faucet
to mix your Shop-Rite ice tea
in a Molly Pitcher.

When you drift toward the idea
of infants being tossed into fires
and children begging for mercy,
try lying in front of the television
with some ice cream, or open up
that long ignored brochure on
how to choose a college for
your growing one-year-old. Time
passes quickly so you better
get on it before your money goes
to the wrong places.

There comes a time
when a question and a fact
become one. There are moments
when every single building
in Sarajevo are felled, and
two come down in New York.
A war on terror is discussed
over Sunday brunch at a local
country club. As you tip your
slender glass under the mimosa fountain,
you wonder what fact remains,
and which sustain.

First Husband

There was no way to see
The day he became either
Too hostile or too helpless.
Either way, you found yourself
Running
From the one who knew all your secrets.
He liked your best friend,
Or landed her.
Or hated her
Because he couldn't.
He helped you run from
A parent's heavy hand,
Your heavy heart,
Until you found your way
Inside. You led
Each other out of one darkness
Into another you hadn't bargained for:

His name seemed to provide
Anonymity from all you were:
The zit-covered teen,
Or the one who sniffed coke
Between geometry and world studies;
He was the skinny, bullied kid
Or grew a mustache later.
He was the homecoming King
Whose parents didn't give a shit,
And whose lucrative sales job
Made no one proud.
The first husband isn't anomalous,
He's you. He's you,
He's you.

Sisters

How much I love my sisters! The countless times we've spent—
hours and years in dramatic, dogged competitions over our hair,
underwear, stealing and hiding what relics we craved
from one another, until screaming fights and fits would brush
the edge of calamity. It's hard to notice diamonds that shine
from all that time polishing what you meant to strike;

How would we know any better? Hormones poised, ready to strike
in a war over the TV channel, the time we spent
fighting outlasted the show; later in life Mitz admitted she'd shine
her shoe soles with my toothbrush if I won. Once I pulled her hair
down to the floor as she bit my wrist to the bone—because of a brush
she wanted that was off limits to sisters who crave

And rant and rave for things that aren't theirs. And why crave
things that aren't yours? Because it's sister's! She ready to strike
you for seizing what wasn't yours—exciting taking! The brush

incident ended with mom hitting the both of us. We spent
years in therapy pondering and pulling out our hair
for mom's reactions to our lives. Later, with a shine

in our eyes, teeth bared, we'd laugh at those battles, that shine
glistening to tears of sadness, self-pity or joy. "From cradle to crave"
I used to say. All we ever did was want—we stopped pulling hair
but pulled other things, other strings. If we could strike
out on our own, surely something'd change! Instead we spent
our first relationships in the same fights, different players. After a brush

with fate, Tania spoke and we realized that toothbrush
was in all our mouths. We no longer felt the need to outshine
each other when one of us divorced—the other two spent
loving hours and years moving her to another craving.
We became honored to help, missions we would gladly strike
out to achieve for each other. Funny, I guard my hair

brush and nail polish when they come over still, but braid their hair
or supply a nurturing facemask or meal, even discuss my brush
with death and other private matters to share. I'll only strike
back when sharing isn't voluntary. I admit an evil streak did shine
this Easter at mom's when Mitz washed laundry there. I craved
her underwear in spite of my older self, and she spent

months asking about them. My hair stands to see it rise and shine still—the inner thief: a childish brush of desire for what you crave— always evading a sister's strike; love and longing forever spent.

Procedure

It was time for surgery—you were sure:
your doctor said your uterus was a liability
and there was no cure
for those fibroids—those black, bloody orbits,
enlarging your varicose veins as if they
were raw radio cords—
twisted purples and pea-green protrusions
of confused wire.

It was a routine cutting, as they go.
They drugged your body down
as we waited and worried,
loitering in the hospital lobby
with TV bolted to ceiling, and cold coffee.
They wheeled you down a hallway
and left you to wake up.
We found you snaked up with IVs, limp,
without your airs, impositions, life.

In all the years I wished you weren't
my mother, seeing you this way I stood
martyred—wishing it wasn't you lying
here, your head cocked back over the pillow,
mouth agape like a nutcracker
yet so, so silent and open.
Hearing no familiar reproach rearranged my
memories—I fell from somewhere
to all the music you made: your fun loving
smile, your passion for the ocean, for a joke,
for my father. I saw you then:
the place where I grew in you
removed; your quiet stillness said
I absolutely loved you.

Patterns

They seemed to agree
there was something special
about their celibacy. It seemed
more spiritual, like when they
read together, he'd quietly
hand her a section of the
Times. Or when they'd shower,
and wash each other's backs.
It went from insatiable licking
to licking the envelopes
of holiday and thank-you
cards; a deeper understanding
of need. They could count
on each other to listen,
about things such as
people not comprehending
trees; only last year,

Joyce Kilmer's came down
in Mahwah for an A&P!
They talked about starting a
petition, invented agendas: Alanon
Wednesdays at 7:00, hypnotherapy
on Fridays—to change their patterns.
They were open to each other
about everything—as long
as they concentrated on
growing, together, everything
would naturally fall.
They began to read more,
and fill each other in
on what they'd learned. This
is what marriage is,
and they knew it.

Kuwait

There's no way to prepare for being a country so little:
you're a snowflake in the wind, flying fragile and focused
anywhere but where you will melt. In Iraq, the fiery, red sun
beat loudly against dusty roads, homes, lineage and locusts,
swarming and hissing like Lockheed
fighter jets flying sleekly over unsuspecting Earth,

traveling in droves towards a corner of Earth
where people scamper under their shadows. Little
is heard above the creatures swooping down, like Lockheed
planes identifying targets—totally focused
on crushing, teeth painted on each aircraft—simulating locusts.
A child plays outside and looks at the sun

and squints immediately. Imagine then, 20 suns,
with airplanes in their wake, circling a helpless Earth—
mothers and fathers powerless to locusts
eating, destroying, eliminating their children. Little

minds cannot process this reality, why any focus
to harm should be on them? Who is Lockheed,

who are behind those wings, why is Lockheed
rolling out planes that are blitzkrieging everything including the sun?
That's how the children saw the sky. If they focused
at all, it was on white blindness—the Earth
shone like a diamond in the night—CNN showed it first, little
rockets like toys curving on the dark screen, locusts

intent on total ruin—government-funded corporate locusts
who were victors in no time. There was a banquet held by Lockheed
with carved ice that even the Chairman attended. Little
hors d'oeuvres were offered by an adroit, brown man named Samson,
whose nametag featured a black bomber gliding high above Earth.
He felt a strange knowledge at this function, awkwardly focused

on a platter of paté made from goose liver; he witnessed the focused
throng of middle managers around a tall, green-suited governor; locusts
smiling with shrimps curled dead and red in their hands. Earth
was aflame a world away as they partied into the evening. Lockheed
celebrated the lottery of having evaded radar first while a son
endured the merriment with metal in his neck. Elsewhere, a girl took a little

charred doll and buried it with her mother. Samson focused on the Lockheed caviar cart dutifully. Locusts were everywhere—smearing the sun from a country's face, then re-lighting Earth, so much fire to save little Kuwait.

Where Are You Headed?

I.

As you drive,
your sweet, traveling mood
gives way to focusing on your hands
holding the steering wheel.
So you don't notice the vast
purple meadows that have silently passed
your window in a haze—like so many things.

Ignoring the fiery magnificence
of a setting sun,
you glimpse a time when you played
in the sand at the end of your driveway.
You thought this was a place you could stay.
How many snug nights in your bed
did you wonder what it would be like
to live in the year 2000?

You have been taken here,
a place you never dreamed,
to decisions which weigh on your chest—
oh, how you thought it could only be easy
you would always be as breezy
and preserved as that kid
who caught Japanese beetles
in a Ziploc bag and curiously
watched them squirm.

You remember golden days
swimming in the warm sea,
Christmas Eves and drinking wine,
trusting a friend, your first "I love you,"
spoken with a passion that could not end.
Now there's a constant blue void
and you drive to a bridge
as you find yourself saying
"Where are you headed?"

II.

The wind on the water
swirls up to you
whispering ideas that crystallize
your heart. It opens a cavern

where you see that it's been only you
who has noticed how strong you've been.
Tiredly you reflect on the birthday
when mom slapped you and screamed
at you to blow out the candles.

You think how death is a joke
in the face of all your accomplishments
and your heart feels a lick
of no recourse, passing through the terrors
of conscious thought. You see your name,
errors, convictions—never captured
in a photograph.
Numbing you, the wind hisses
and you see a picture now—
you're standing on a bridge.

You put away all things special—
they slip and snap out of sight.
You look down
and then straight ahead
to the intangible horizon
and then look up
to the inconsolable sky
feeling yourself slipping

knowing you are about to fall
your face hardens like a soldier's
the lines in your forehead
spreading out into a blank stare
before you give it all up—
the tears, the godawful loneliness
of no one understanding,
the exhaustion and anguish of watching
your only good moments evolve
into parched, crumpled autumn leaves
and blow away.
Then you go.

III.

It's winter, your realization,
and, as you fall,
you know it will all be gone
relief is imminent
and you don't care
about who you're going to hurt
because they'll get over it someday
and you're resentful even to them

that they couldn't help you
as you fall

and just at that last moment
when you thanklessly blacken to God,
you wish for a millisecond
that you could have had the strength.

Postcard

I stare at the sea
as the far away steamships
glide effortlessly across
the horizon. I long for you
as a seed wants up to the sun;
if I could reach, feel you here,
if I could break time like glass
and make you appear.

The walls are clay all around
me. Clocktowers clang
the minutes and days our
bodies won't unite. A gull
ascends high into a yellowing sky,
her powers to defy time
towards her beloved.

What are we, staring
into our hands in our different
chairs, mine in front of grey,
turning water and you,
with a mountain of leafless trees
overseeing your moving to
clear the breakfast dishes
in the early dawn light?

They wait in their roots
like glad witnesses,
ready to receive a bird
or a breeze or a misting
from above. The window
fogs beyond my face: we watch
with them. We wait.

Peruvian-Yugoslavian-Italian-American

Being born in America, yet not exactly American, heritage
has been a conundrum from the start: like wearing shoes
that aren't yours—they fit, but they don't. Their roots
are someone else's or something else's—an idea, a desire
to be cast in a mold, in a culture that thrives on being
the consumer nationality. One light

shines on all of us, a kind of neon, blinding spotlight
that is flipped on if we try to live out one true heritage—
it's always slippery to see who is the one being
the bearer of this light; who's shoes
we're really walking in, what our desires
really are, for ourselves, for our families, for our roots.

My roots
are Peruvian-Yugoslavian-Italian-American. A light-
skinned father and an olive-skinned mother. Her one desire

for my whole life has been to hide her heritage—
to blend in as an immigrant, to wear the shoes
of her business peers, to pass off as being

French; being
French, after all, affords one the roots
of a snob culture, or so it has been said. My shoes
are occupied with awkward feet, an untrained gait I wish was light;
in layers behind my husband and daughter I wear my heritage—
their red hair, blue eyes, yet my desire

for her to be bilingual. My desire
for her to have Abuelita and Nona in one house. Being
white, arguably, has its costs. In America, heritage
has to be lost to be gained. Roots
are re-rooted, and re-routed, and re-rooted again, a light
load getting heavier with a confused notion of whose shoes

we really want to fill. I want my daughter's hand-me-down shoes
from her cousins to be a sign of love, not economy. If her desire
is to be herself, not a version of a heritage cast down like a light,
then something is being
done right. Today I uproot my roots,
long overdue—an adult re-seeing her heritage

in working-class thrift store shoes and being
damn proud of it. My desire is for everyone's roots
to be honored: our God-given right to shed light on our heritage!

Corporate Epiphany #365

The day of my divorce,
I was asked to return from the courthouse
and work a 16-hour day.
I did.
The week I put in for vacation,
I was asked to work through it to
meet a deadline.
I did.
When my sister delivered her baby breach,
I was asked to stay until the end of the day
like everybody else.
I did.
When my grandmother died,
I was asked to return to work after
three mourning days.
I did.
That blizzard in 1997 when the

government declared our area a disaster,
I was asked to record that absence
as a personal day.
I did.
During my annual review,
I was told I didn't "walk the talk,"
due to the fact that I asked for that
vacation during a deadline.
Sign the form, they said, no raise.
I did.

One evening on the local news,
it was reported that a man walked calmly
into a brokerage house and pulled
a pistol from each suit pocket
like John Wayne and began
blowing heads off.

Think he was crazy?
I didn't.

Crossing Over Loss

(for Lyz)

He could never imagine what he'd be famous
for. He would not have gone
anywhere but home if he had the choice
to be a hero in death or the adored
husband, son, father, he still
is. Only not here.

Here,
A wife, mother, daughter makes herself famous
in his memory. She copes in public while still
grieving, always in disbelief that he's gone,
always feeling she'll wake up to her adored
lover and all their choices,

their choice
to live on the water, to hear
the surf outside the house they adored,

those early hours so famous
to her now for his being gone
as the sun rises; the still

air against her cheek. Their child still
in the cradle beside her, awakening: her choice
to always have her near. A year gone
by is inconceivable: here
is proof of his life, his famous
face on his child, who cannot be more adored

than while crossing over loss. The adored
cannot be more missed than now. She still
hears his voice in certain moments. Famous
luminaries work for glory by choice:
how could it have happened here?
How could he really be gone?

The crossing is lifelong, expansive. The gone
only answer in fitful dreams. She feels adored
just before sleep eases her to a place far from here,
where all the most beautiful illusions still
hold a place in her life, her choices
for her family unfamous

and calmly familiar. Did she feel his touch? Oh, he is gone, still:
all she ever adored in changed circumstances. Her choice
to cross transforms her from here to famous, while all watch in awe.

Go

You gave me a ticket to the Caribbean
saying we should get away again, your
intrinsic desire to explore, telling me not to
worry anymore about my bills or about my loved
ones who mutilate themselves or about my father
hiding from the FBI.
Let's just go for two weeks you said, bringing me
more roses while I cried in bed, *you'll be happy
when you see those white beaches and palm trees.*
So I conceded, feeling anyone would be crazy not to
jump for a chance like this. I packed some things,
looked at your brochures, and decided in the
face of all this bliss that I wouldn't go.
Almost fazed by my abundance of tears, my
I just can't anymores, my gasps into each tissue
you placed in front of my dripping nose,
my wails of *I'm depleted, dry, and I don't mean to*

let you down after all these years but please gos,
you went on—early the next morning leaving the
note *I love you, I'm not mad and hope things get
better with your dad—*
in your orderly way that leaves me blinking
and staring.

I sit on the dock and hug myself, knowing I needed
to stay. I breathe the muddy air of the lake day after
day, feeling you in my gut like an oyster's grit.
In the fact of my body missing yours, things soften.
We exist in different climates. You don't check in
with a call.
I sit. I measure; I take in the fall. Witnessing the
weather and how it seethes, what it does to the once
green leaves makes me a leaf, too. They blow
around me in browns and would grow wings
if they could to fly towards you.
They land on the shimmering black, wet and face
up, beckoning to me in small waves, as if
trying to tell me something I may already know.
Deep inside the blackness of me a seed
of something, an inherence, prepares to
grow.

Lakeside, Month Eight

You move every day now.
With each kick,
a new step taken: fingers
part, cellophane nails
rise over pink skin;
eyes flutter; ears listen. A fish
in a dark lake, you're in a place
of no doubt—cradled, feeding,
breathing, unfree; and you
don't want to be.

It is warm.
I laugh into the sunset
while the moon appears
over me. All of us are accepted
into the lake's large, watchful,
watery eye.

As dusk ushers the stars into sight,
I sigh upon the knowledge of you,
ready for the world like the Heron
fanning the water in flight,
stretching its neck
towards eternity.

Spring Lake

Green wood floats by
the dock, under moving shadows
of reaching leaves, leaves reaching
for mountains and clouds
and the noiseless life
around the March-thawed lake.
The ice glides in pieces
to the right by the warm wind,
waving the grass, the grass
and its shady harbor—
the place for the pike.

This is where she lays her eggs:
centered once she chooses
her spot; she does not move
from her shadow, the shadows
of the moving grass, or the

shadow of the oak—looming
above with approving moves,
leaves like green hands
blessing the life, the receding ice,
the pike over her bulbous jelly
pile—waiting to spring forth
like seeds, like trees, like
leaves—born from darkness
into light.

About the Author

Lorraine Stanchich is the daughter of Peruvian and Yugoslavian/Italian immigrants. She began writing when she was eight years old. Ms. Stanchich teaches writing and literature in New Jersey, most recently as an adjunct professor of Humanities and Poetry at Ramapo College of New Jersey, and as a tutor of English. An exuberant nature lover and triathlete, she lives with her husband and daughter in northern New Jersey. She answers e-mail at: l@landoflorraine.com.

About the Artist

Michael Grosso received a doctorate in Philosophy from Columbia University and has taught for over twenty years. He lives in rural New York where he facilitates philosophical cafés and likes to gaze from his window at the Shawangunk Mountains. The cover painting, "The Third Eye," was painted in 1999. To inquire about his work, e-mail mgrosso@warwick.net.